LESSONS LEARNED
ON THE CORNER IN KALIHI

LESSONS LEARNED

ON THE CORNER IN KALIHI

by
WESLEY T. PARK

WATERMARK
PUBLISHING

ISBN 0-9753740-3-6

Library of Congress Control Number:
2004116213

Printed in the United States of America

Design and production by
OSHIRO DESIGN

WATERMARK PUBLISHING
1088 Bishop Street, Suite 310
Honolulu, HI 96813
TELEPHONE: Toll-free 1-866-900-BOOK
E-MAIL: sales@bookshawaii.net
WEB SITE: www.bookshawaii.net

For Wintehn, Ku'uhaku and Kamalu.

Pass on, no pass back.

————————————————

*Special thanks to Michael Kimura,
Raleigh Awaya, Clara Yamamoto and Glenn Sexton
for logistical support.*

*And to Duane Kurisu for including me in his quest
to retain the local values we grew up with.*

THE BOYS ON THE CORNER, KALIHI, 1953

*Charley-boy, Big Shot, Peʻa, Jerry, Rudy, Rawley, Sonny,
Dike, Feet, Alan, Charley, Mel, Uku, Bobby, Mitsu,
Buddy, Toʻi, Willie, Roy and German.*

FOREWORD

BY WALTER A. DODS, JR.
Chairman of the Board, First Hawaiian Bank

My friendship with Wesley Park goes back a long way—not quite as far as his Kalihi youth, but more than 30 years. In that time, he has had a successful career in business and on campus. *Lessons Learned on the Corner in Kalihi* demonstrates that he did so while holding on to the values—and the friendships—of his childhood.

Wes Park has friends from the roughest, toughest parts of our society as well as in Hawai'i's corporate boardrooms. He's at home with anybody, anywhere, because he has lived by the values he lays out in this book.

Undoubtedly he was thinking of himself when he wrote, on page 145, "Appreciate people who tell you jokes." Over the years, nobody has told me more jokes than Wes. While it's also true that nobody has told me more bad jokes, he has indeed brought laughter into my life countless times.

The bad jokes are one of the crosses his wife, Daphne, has had to bear over the years. Fortunately for her, Wes spends more of the time living out the other wise sayings here than he does as a humorist.

"When you give, give with your heart," Wes writes on page 19. This book, which shares his wonderful outlook on life, is Wes Park's gift to us all. He's the local boy's local boy and my friend.

Wes has taught me a lot by example. This book teaches us all that a few well-chosen words can have power.

Mahalo, Wes.

———

Hawaiʻi, like anywhere else, has its own unique local ways. These traditions have been shaped by several important elements that make the local culture distinctive.

- Ours is an inclusive culture, one that does not discriminate by race or religion. It is possible for newcomers to be excluded, however, if they don't buy into that culture.

- A spirit of racial acceptance among local people permits open, good-natured teasing and joking about our ethnic differences.

- Each ethnic group in Hawaiʻi can be divided into three separate groups: foreign nationals, mainland guys and local guys. The local culture welcomes people from all three groups, so long as they subscribe to local values.

- Because the local culture is an island culture, and because we all live in such close proximity, personal relationships and caring for one another are of paramount importance.

- At the very core of local culture is the Native Hawaiian culture, with its powerful guiding principle of aloha.

Lessons Learned on the Street Corner in Kalihi is the author's way of passing along to his children and their children the essence of local culture—lessons he in turn learned from his parents, his grandparents, his wife, Daphne Marie Hokuaoʻonalani Park, and his friends.

Hawaiʻi's "local boy" culture is a blend of many diverse ethnic influences, but the end result is a set of universally accepted standards admired in most cultures. The author believes that if the people of a culture accept and under-stand themselves—warts and all—they can then better understand and appreciate people of other cultures.

The thoughts and sayings in these pages are a personal guide, expressed in simple everyday terms, for living in peace with oneself while fitting comfortably into the local culture. The book was originally planned as just two copies, one for each of the author's children. But friends who helped print them felt that a book reflecting local values, written by a local person, should be more widely distributed. George Engebretson and the people at Watermark Publishing have published this expanded edition, in keeping with the AIO Group's ongoing mission to preserve our local ways for future generations.

It is the author's sincere hope that readers will use the thoughts and sayings here to search within themselves—for insights into their own values, principles and "local ways."

Every day is a gift. Enjoy it.

Once the day is gone you can never get it back.

All human beings make mistakes.
So forgive them, starting with
yourself.

People who don't know, don't know that they don't know, so they think they know.

Doing the small things right prepares
us to do the BIG things right.

It is not who is right but what is right.

1. Know where you want to go.

2. Think two steps ahead.

3. Make Plan A, Plan B and Plan C.

4. *Focus.*

5. Have *discipline* to do what you have to do to get the job done.

Life is simple.

When you're down, pick yourself up.

When you're high, don't let yourself
get carried away.

For everything you want there is
a price.

Be sure to know what that price is
before you get what you want.

When you accept, accept with your heart, and never forget about the gift and the giver.

(See page 19.)

When you give, give with your heart,
then forget about it.

(See page 17.)

Never invest money with anyone
wearing alligator shoes.

(See the previous page.)

Don't try to figure out who you are all the time. Instead, spend your time figuring out who you want to become and work towards that goal.

Positive things happen to people
who think positive.

Forgetting junk stuff helps you to be happy.

Old friends are the best friends
because they are proven.

Try not to take things too personally.

People often act weird around you because they have other problems on their minds, which usually have nothing to do with you.

When you feel good, don't think too much. Just enjoy it.

Not everyone is into friendship.

If you lose a friend, chances are he or she wasn't a true friend to begin with.

It's OK to like or love someone even though they don't like or love you.

Just don't make a fool of yourself.

Everybody needs space for themselves at times.

Structure your life so that you have some time alone.

Also, give the people around you space when they need it.

People show their true character in two situations:

1. When things are going super great (especially when there is money, power or glory involved)

2. When they see things falling into failure for themselves and they feel that their backs are against the wall

Sometimes, people resent others
who have helped them to gain
success because they like to believe
that they did it all by themselves.

Live your life so that you will be
seen as being a kind person by those
you love.

Don't gamble in your own hometown and don't drink before the sun goes down.

When you are really worried about something that might happen—do two things.

First, imagine the worst possible outcome and decide what you would do to cope with the situation in order to survive.

Second, then expect the best.

That way you're ready for the worst, but you're not screwed up, because you're anticipating good results.

Reality is usually skewed towards the middle between the worst and the best.

Never buy anything from a salesman
with greasy hair and a thin mustache.

Listen closely to what people are saying but also watch what they are doing.

Many people are naive because they have good ears but have bad eyes.

Loyalty between friends must be 100%.

Even if people are disloyal only 1% of the time, that 1% disloyalty can pop out at any time

So always be on guard with those who are not 100% loyal all the time.

What is loyalty between friends?

Loyalty between friends is no matter what—right or wrong.

A loyal friend will say, "that's my friend."

That's all.

In order to change results you must change the cause of the results.

Random acts of kindness are only
fully appreciated by kind people.

For any group of people to advance, one generation must be willing to sacrifice for the next.

Your spouse should be your best friend.

Children are God's gifts to us.

Do thoughtful things for your loved ones; thank them and love them while they are still living.

Don't cry with regrets at the funeral that you "should have."

Except for physical violence, let your children fight their own battles.

It will make them stronger people.

Love your children unconditionally.

Let them know that you always love *them* even when you are not happy with their *actions*.

Give your best efforts to raising your children because you only have one shot at each stage of their lives. There are no second chances.

Men and women who seek money, glory or power for their own sake will never achieve their goals and will always remain unhappy and unfulfilled.

There never seems to be enough of anything for these people.

In the social world, don't try to reach too far from where you're raised.

Never overreach to where you're uncomfortable.

When you entertain, never try to impress your guests; invite nice people only, and serve what you enjoy and can afford.

When starting a business, make sure
you have enough capital to see you
through not only the start-up but
also the future bad times.

Successful management is getting to the point where you're spending time preventing problems rather than reacting to problems.

Commitments are made with a
handshake.

Kindness is not to be mistaken for weakness.

Do the right thing, no matter how inconvenient or unpopular it may seem.

Don't let others with negative attitudes take the joy out of your life.

Celebrate the little victories.

Take care of the people who work for you, for you have a great effect on them and their loved ones.

People who think they are big shots often develop this ability: when anyone blows smoke up their okoles, it goes straight to their heads.

Doctors call it the anal cranial tube.

When you are young and struggling, it seems like you have to pay retail for everything.

As you get older and more affluent, so do your friends, and you get good deals when you could afford to pay retail.

Cigars should be smoked in solitude.

Never eat at a restaurant that
advertises its view and not its food.

Only collect art that you enjoy being around.

Speak positively.

It will force you to think positively, and ultimately to be a positive person.

Be happy for other people's good fortunes.

In your heart you will be a happier person because others' good luck will be yours too.

When all is sad and dark, look to God for joy and light.

Let light represent God and get out of the dark, both in your mind and in your eyes.

Look for sunlight or any kind of light to get out of the dark, literally and figuratively.

To be happy:

Enjoy and appreciate the heck out of all that you have, and don't grouse over what you don't have.

We often don't appreciate what we have until we lose it.

Don't believe everything you hear or read.

Everybody has biases—some big, some small.

Remember, where they stand often depends on where they sit.

Telling lies obscures the memory, because you have to remember double:

You have to remember the truth and the lie.

So while it might be difficult at times, always tell the truth.

When you don't toot your own horn, others will take the credit. But you will have the true satisfaction of knowing that you made a contribution, even though nobody else does.

If you don't have large problems,
your small problems often appear to
be large.

Once the glass is full, it will always be perceived later as half empty rather than half full.

The challenge then is how to make the most of half a glass.

Try not to waste time and effort on revenge; it's drudgery and weighs heavily on the soul.

Just remember what goes around comes around, and vice versa—the good and the bad.

Anger and hatred bounce right back
at the sender in many different ways.

The good thing about having an enemy unjustly going around saying bad things about you is that you find out by their reactions who your real friends are.

Having so many people stick up for you is always a pleasant surprise.

Every individual can beat you at something.

That is one of the reasons you should never feel superior and look down your nose at any one.

(See page 135.)

You can beat any individual at at least one thing.

That is the reason you should never have to bow down to anyone or kiss okole.

(See page 133.)

Some people cannot handle success.

They get puffed up with their own importance and forget whom they are supposed to serve.

Stay away from them.

To live with honor you have to be willing to die for honor—many little deaths day to day.

You don't have to express an opinion all the time to be honest.

Silence is sometimes the best opinion.

If someone does not like you, don't try to be his or her friend.

Have as little contact as possible.

Appreciate people who tell you jokes.

They are trying to bring laughter into your life.

Old books, old jokes and old songs
are like old friends.

Kindness is the best human trait.

Spitefulness is the worst human trait.

Grow old with grace and dignity.
Don't fight it.

You never finish paying your dues.

PAU